ALLAN RAMSAY (1686-1758)
was a Scottish poet born in Leadhills,
Lanarkshire in 1686 and educated in
neighbouring Crawford. He wrote
poetry in Scots and English as well as
working as a publisher, a bookseller,
and a wig maker. Allan Ramsay was
a founding member, and eventually
club laureate, of the Easy Club.
He was also a playwright, and founded
a theatre in Edinburgh's Carruber's
Close. His shop near the Luckenbooths
was Britain's first circulating library.
Ramsay gathered together the
sayings of Scotland as *A Collection
of Scots Proverbs*, first published in
the 18th century.

Ye'll no sell your hen on a rainy day

...and other canny Scottish proverbs

Collected by
ALLAN RAMSAY

Selected by
LUATH PRESS

Luath Press Limited

EDINBURGH

www.luath.co.uk

First published 2018

ISBN: 978-1-910745-39-7

Proverbs sourced from:
A Collection of Scots Proverbs,
more complete and correct than heretofore published
by Allan Ramsay, published by Allan Ramsay,
Edinburgh, 1739

The paper used in this book is recyclable. It is made
from low chlorine pulps produced in a low energy,
low emission manner from renewable forests.

Printed and bound by T.J. International, Padstow

Design by Tom Bee

Typeset in Mayflower by 3btype.com

CONTENTS

FAMILY

Birth's good but breeding's better

Hard work can make up for a bad start

Ill bairns are best heard at hame

*Badly behaved children are best
appreciated in private,
rather than inflicted on strangers*

Dawted bairns
do bear little

*Mollycoddled children
grow up to become
useless adults*

Speak good of pipers, your father was a fiddler

It is difficult to appreciate the talents of your parents

Maiden's bairns
are aye
well bred

*People without children
always think they know best
when it comes to parenting*

What's in yer wame is no in yer testament

*If you live well and eat well,
you won't have much to leave
to your children*

That's the piece a step-bairn never got

That is the best part of something

Your head will never fill your father's bonnet

You are not as a good a man as your father

Burnt bairns
dread fire

*Let your children make their
own mistakes*

Never seek a wife
till ye ken
what to do with her

*Don't marry until you're ready
for the responsibility*

WORK

An idle brain is the devil's workshop

*If you work hard and keep busy,
you are better placed to
resist temptations*

Corn him well and he'll work the better

*If you pay people what they deserve,
they will work harder
for you*

He'll no let grass grow at his heels

*He works hard
and keeps himself busy*

Hand in use
is father of lair

*You learn things most effectively by
actually doing them*

Diligence is the mother of good luck

Luck is an illusion; those who put the effort in get the best results

Ye'll no hurry yourself with your ain hands

*You will work harder
if you are being supervised*

Better keep well than make well

There is no point in working so hard that you make yourself ill

Ye're good enough but ye're no braw enough

You meet the requirements for the job, but you're nothing special

It keeps his nose at the grindstone

It keeps him busy

Do what you ought come what will

Spend your life doing something that is important to you

Ye're sair fash'd hadding neathing together

You're working extremely hard but spreading yourself too thinly and achieving nothing

Mony hands make light work

*Working together
makes a task easier on everyone*

PERSONALITIES

He's no sae daft
as he lets on

*He acts the fool
but he's got a hidden agenda*

She hauds up her head like a hen drinking water

She is extremely vain and proud

He kens whilk side his cake is buttered on

He know where his advantages lie

Great barkers are nae biters

Those who are loud with their threats are not likely to carry them out

A blate cat
makes a proud mouse

*It is wrong to feel proud about
outwitting a stupid opponent*

She looks as if butter would not melt in her mou'

She appears gentle and innocent but she is probably not

Like the cur in the crub, he'll neither do nor let up

He won't get the job done,
but he won't shut up about it either

He has meikle prayer
but little devotion

*He asks for a lot but
shows little commitment himself*

A taking hand
will never want

If you are willing to accept help,
then you will be better off

A hungry man's aye angry

Be aware that people may be short-tempered because of the hardships they face

Ae scabbed sheep will smit the hale hirdsel

One bad person will reflect badly on everyone in their group

There is nane sae bline as them that wadna see

It is easy to ignore what you don't want to see

MONEY

Better go to bed supperless than rise in debt

It is better to suffer a short-term hardship immediately rather than build up larger hardships long-term

A sillerless man gangs fast through the market

*When you are poor,
there is no attraction to seeing
what you cannot have*

Ill payers
are aye good cravers

*People who are not intending to pay
make a lot of demands*

Ye never saw
green cheese
but your e'evn reel'd

You have always been covetous,
and still you want more

Better auld debts
than auld sairs

It is better to owe a friend
some money than fall out with them

Better find iron
than tine siller

*It is better to be profitable
on low-cost goods than to
lose money on expensive ones*

Better a toom house
than an ill tenant

*It is better to rent to no one than
to a tenant who causes you trouble*

Penny wise
and pound foolish

*There is no point in
scrimping and scraping
over small amounts if you are
careless about large purchases*

A fou purse
never lacks friends

*Be wary about people who are only
friendly when you are well off*

Better buy
than barrow

*It is better to pay for something
outright than borrow money for it*

Fools make feasts
and wise men
eat them

*Do not let people take advantage
of your generosity*

A fool and his money
are soon parted

*A foolish person
will not keep money long*

WEATHER

Good can never come from bad

*If something seems like a lost cause,
it probably is one*

It is an ill wind that blaws naebody good

Something bad in general may nevertheless do good for someone

Make your hay
when the sun shines

*Make the most of opportunities
when they occur*

Come with the wind and gae with the water

If something arrives with ease it may also leave with ease

Fancy flees
before the wind

Pay no heed to fleeting desires

Ye'll no sell your hen on a rainy day

There is no point attempting something in unfavourable conditions

Sorrow and ill weather come unsent for

Bad things happen unexpectedly –
Spoken upon the arrival of an
unwanted visitor

A misty morning
may be a clear day

*Don't lose heart
if things start badly,
they may improve later*

SELF-IMPROVEMENT

A bird in the hand
is worth twa
in the bush

It is better to appreciate what you have now than to obsess over what you may have in future

If ye do wrang, make amends

If you do wrong,
do all you can to make it right

Say well's good
but do well is better

Actions speak louder than words

Open confession is good for the saul

Honesty is good for you

Ill will never spake well

When two people don't get along,
take what they say about
one another with a pinch of salt

Give o'er when the play is good

Quit while you're ahead

Well is that well does

*Do good and things are bound
to go well for you*

Diligence is the mother of good luck

Good luck comes from hard work

I'll never dirty the bonnet I'm going to put on

Don't cause trouble close to home, or you'll end up mixed up in it yourself

He that sleeps with dogs maun rise with flaes

The company you keep reflects upon you

FOOD AND DRINK

Sharp stomachs
make short graces

*The needy will not always
bother with politeness*

Hungry dogs
are blithe
of bursthen puddings

Those in need are not picky

Ill beef never
mad good broo

Good will not come from bad

Hunger
is a good kitchen

Wanting something badly
makes it better when it comes

Better a bit
in the morning
than fast a' day

Better to accept a enough than
to hold out for more

Spilt ale is waur than water

There's no point in having something nice if you aren't going to use it right

Drink little that ye may drink lang

It is best to be sparing, so that what you have may last

When drink's in wit's out

Drinking will make you foolish

Evening oats are good morning fodder

Plan for the future and it will turn out well

Everything hath an end and a pudding has twa

All things eventually come to an end

Enough is as good as a feast

Having only what you need is as good as having more

A hungry man's aye angry

One who appears antisocial may be a victim of circumstance

LIFESTYLE
AND
HOUSEHOLD

Hame is hame though it were never so hamely

No matter how humble your dwelling, it is special just for being home

A toom pantry makes a thriftless gudewife

When you have nothing it is hard to be mindful of the future

Fair words winna gar the pot boil

Pretty talk won't get things done

Tine thimble
tane thrift

A task will be completed faster with the correct tools

Welcome
is the best dish
in the kitchen

*Being welcoming is more important
than having fine food to share*

Twa fools in a house are a couple o'er mony

Two fools in a house
is two fools too many

When my head's down my house is theeked

Work hard and your home life will be comfortable

A wee bush is better than nae bield

An insubstantial shelter is better than no shelter at all

His auld brass
will buy a new pan

*Careful what you think of as rubbish,
it may well be worth something*

Sie reek asis therein comes out of the lum top

The truth will always out

HONESTY
AND
LIES

I can scarce
believe you,
you speak sae fair

*Fancy language
often hides something*

He has meikle prayer but little devotion

Those who are the most ostentatiously good may not be what they seem

Sair cravers
are aye ill prayers

The greedy are never godly

What's my case
the day may be yours
the morn

Treat the less fortunate well,
because it could be you tomorrow

A liar should have a good memory

A liar will soon tangle himself up in untruths

Three can keep
a secret if twaw be awa

A secret will always out

An ill plea
should be well pled

*If you are going to lie,
at least do it well*

An ill turn
is soon done

It's all too easy to do wrong

Ane never tines
by doing good

One never loses by doing good

Take a man
by his word
and a cow
by her horn

*It is best to take someone
at their word,
but sometimes it is tough
to hold them to it*

DEATH
AND
ILLNESS

Were it not for hop, heart wad break

We must always have hope

Time
and thinking tame
the strongest grief

Time heals all wounds

As lang lives
the merry man
as the sad

*What happens will happen,
so you may as well spend
your life happy*

We maun live by the living and no by the dead

Focus on what you have, not what you have lost

Young folk may die, but auld folk maun die

Death is possible at any age, and inevitable eventually

Luath Press Limited

committed to publishing well written books worth reading

LUATH PRESS takes its name from Robert Burns, whose little collie Luath (*Gael.*, swift or nimble) tripped up Jean Armour at a wedding and gave him the chance to speak to the woman who was to be his wife and the abiding love of his life.

Burns called one of 'The Twa Dogs' Luath after Cuchullin's hunting dog in Ossian's *Fingal*. Luath Press was established in 1981 in the heart of Burns country, and now resides a few steps up the road from Burns' first lodgings on Edinburgh's Royal Mile.

Luath offers you distinctive writing with a hint of unexpected pleasures.

Most bookshops in the UK, the US, Canada, Australia, New Zealand and parts of Europe either carry our books in stock or can order them for you. To order direct from us, please send a £sterling cheque, postal order, international money order or your credit card details (number, address of cardholder and expiry date) to us at the address below. Please add post and packing as follows: UK – £1.00 per delivery address; overseas surface mail – £2.50 per delivery address; overseas airmail – £3.50 for the first book to each delivery address, plus £1.00 for each additional book by airmail to the same address. If your order is a gift, we will happily enclose your card or message at no extra charge.

Luath Press Limited
543/2 Castlehill
The Royal Mile
Edinburgh EH1 2ND
Scotland

Telephone: 0131 225 4326 (24 hours)
email: sales@luath.co.uk
Website: www.luath.co.uk